Tadpole REX

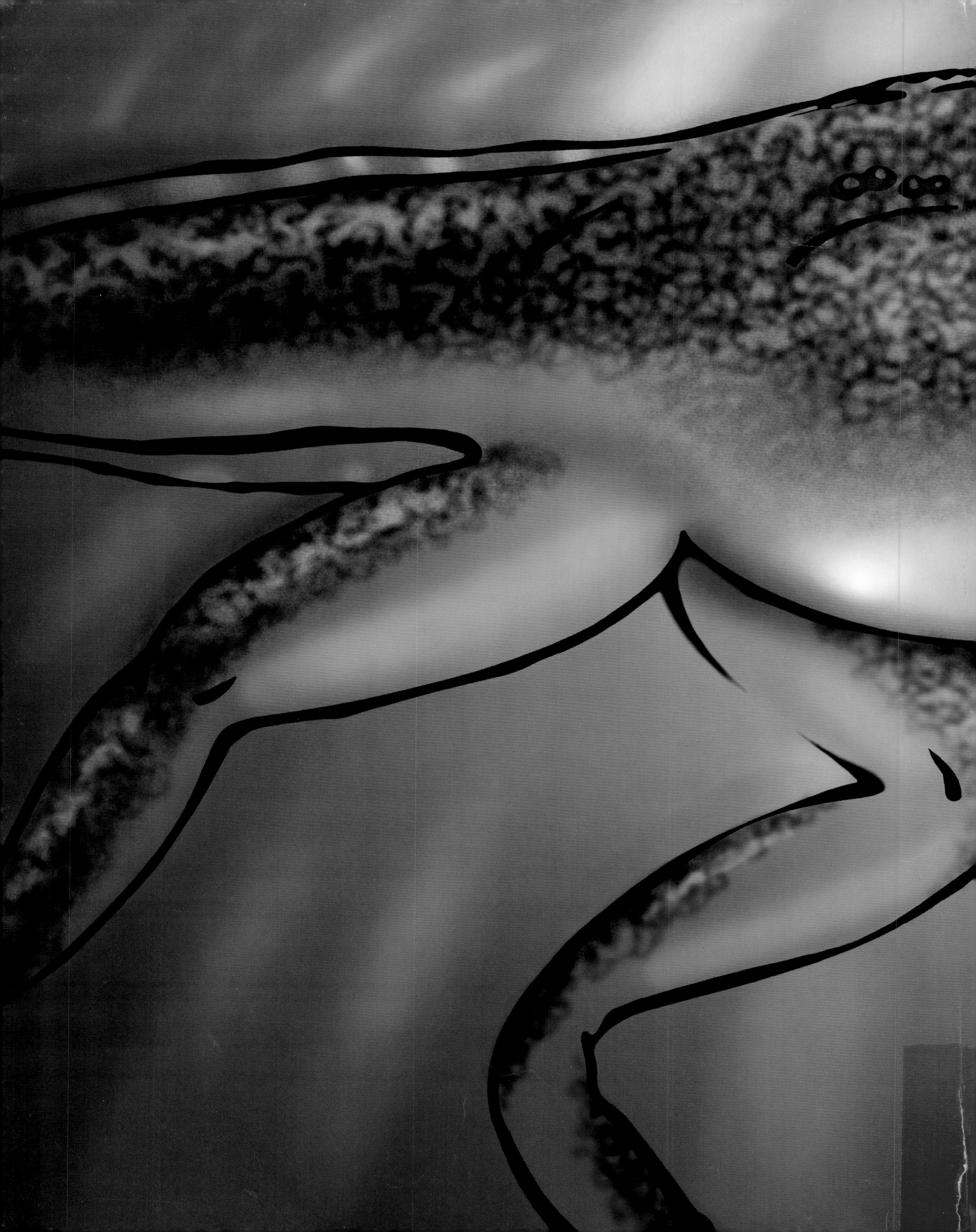

Tadpole REX

BY
KURT CYRUS

HARCOURT, INC.
ORLANDO AUSTIN NEW YORK SAN DIEGO LONDON
MANUFACTURED IN CHINA

Deep in the goop of a long-ago swamp,
a whopping big dinosaur went for a stomp.

Stomp! went the dinosaur. **Squish!** went the goop.

Up came the bubbles—

Bloop.

Bloop.

Bloop.

Swish went the horsetails, tattered and torn.
Then water rushed in . . .

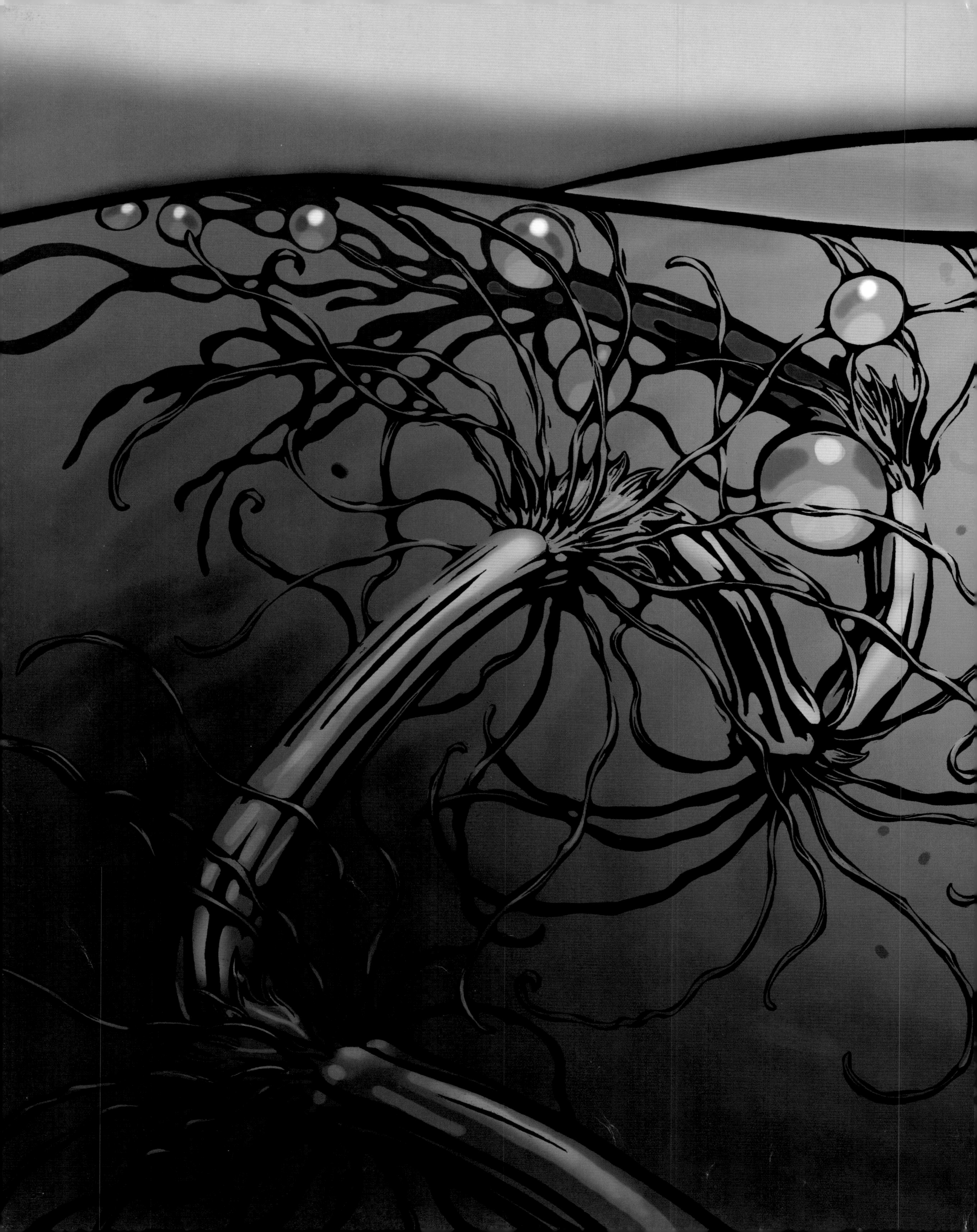

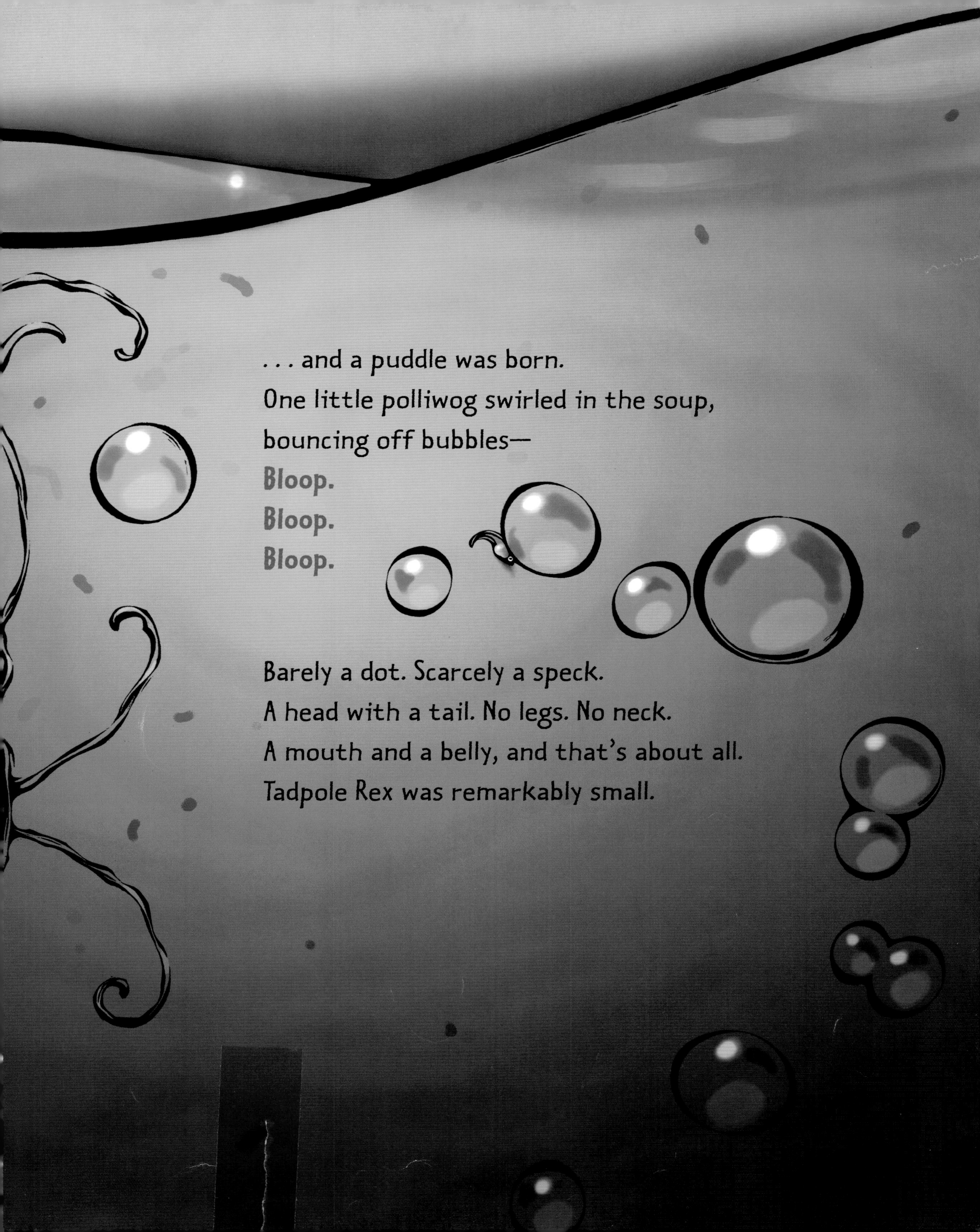

. . . and a puddle was born.
One little polliwog swirled in the soup,
bouncing off bubbles—
Bloop.
Bloop.
Bloop.

Barely a dot. Scarcely a speck.
A head with a tail. No legs. No neck.
A mouth and a belly, and that's about all.
Tadpole Rex was remarkably small.

Primeval puddles were desperate places
of ambush and panic and life-or-death chases.

Stuck in a footprint with nowhere to go,
surrounded by giants, Rex lay low.
Mud was his camouflage. Mud was his friend.
But Rex wouldn't wallow in mud in the end. . . .

For somewhere inside him, deep in his core,
there slumbered an inner tyrannosaur.
A Rex who was fearless, with fire in his blood—

Splash! went a hunter.
Rex hit the mud.

But soon Rex grew,
as tadpoles do.

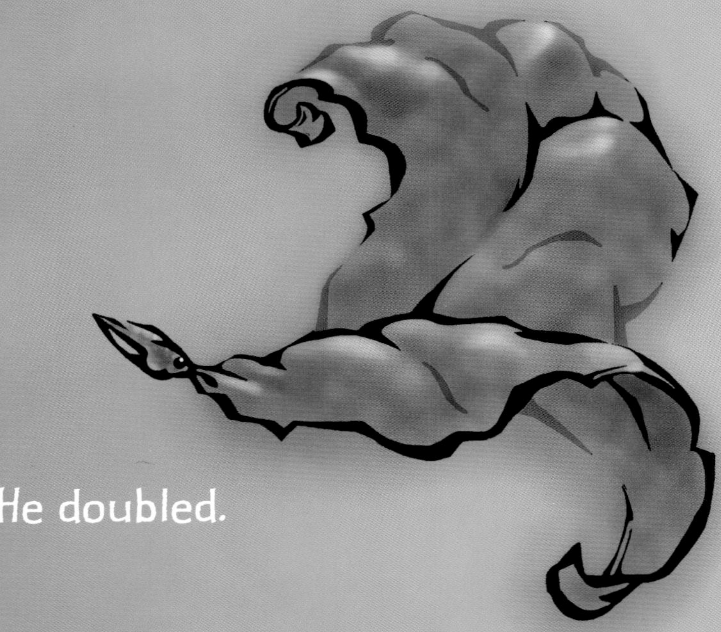

He doubled.

He tripled.

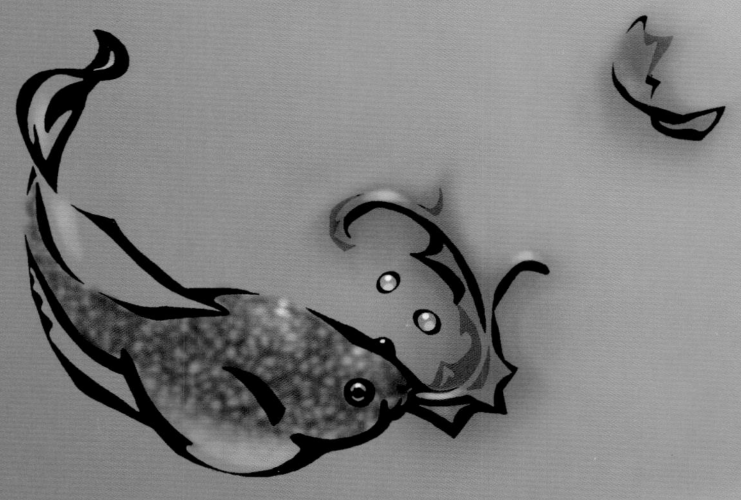

He grew by four.

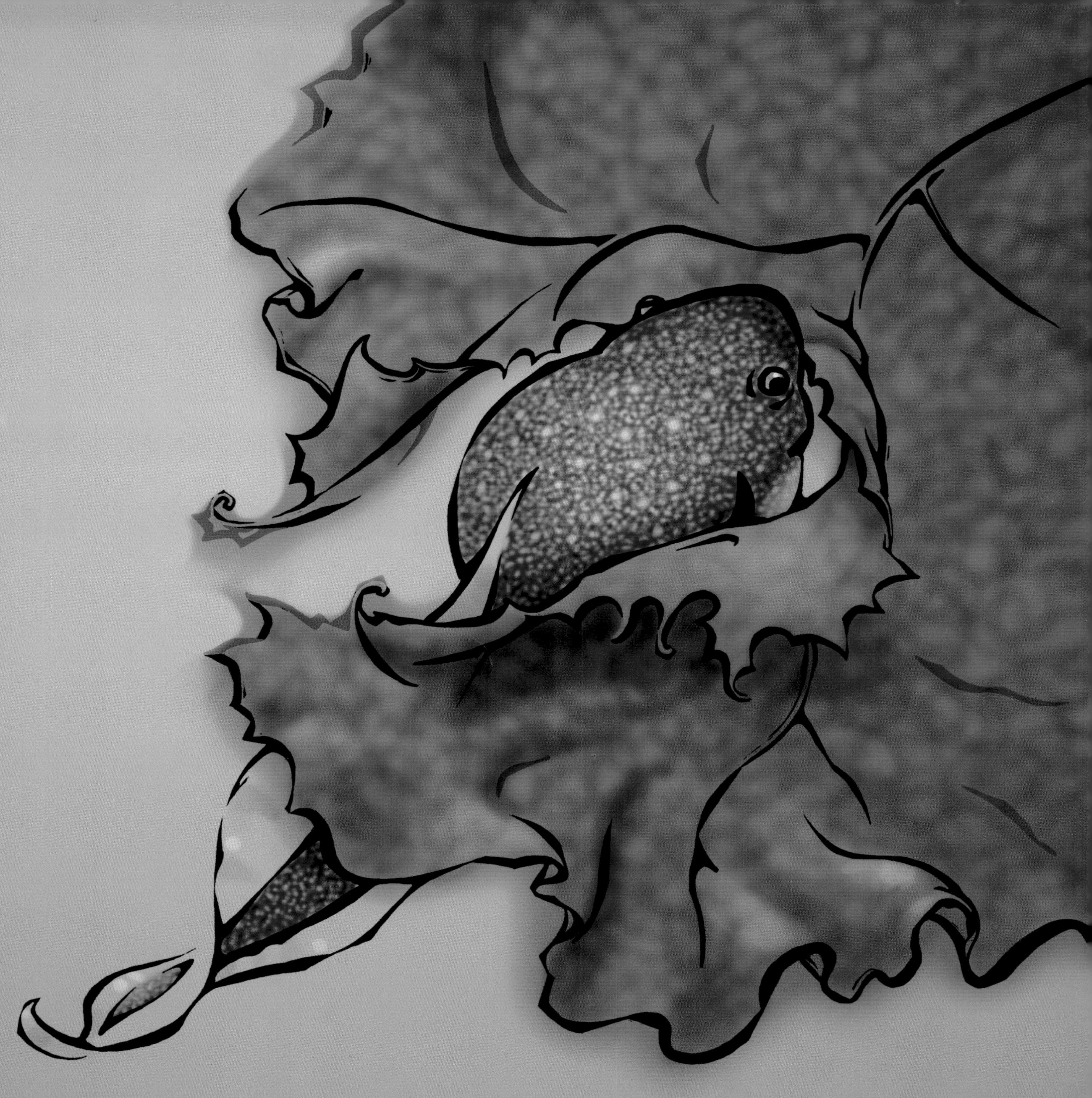

He ate like a hungry tyrannosaur.
And then . . .

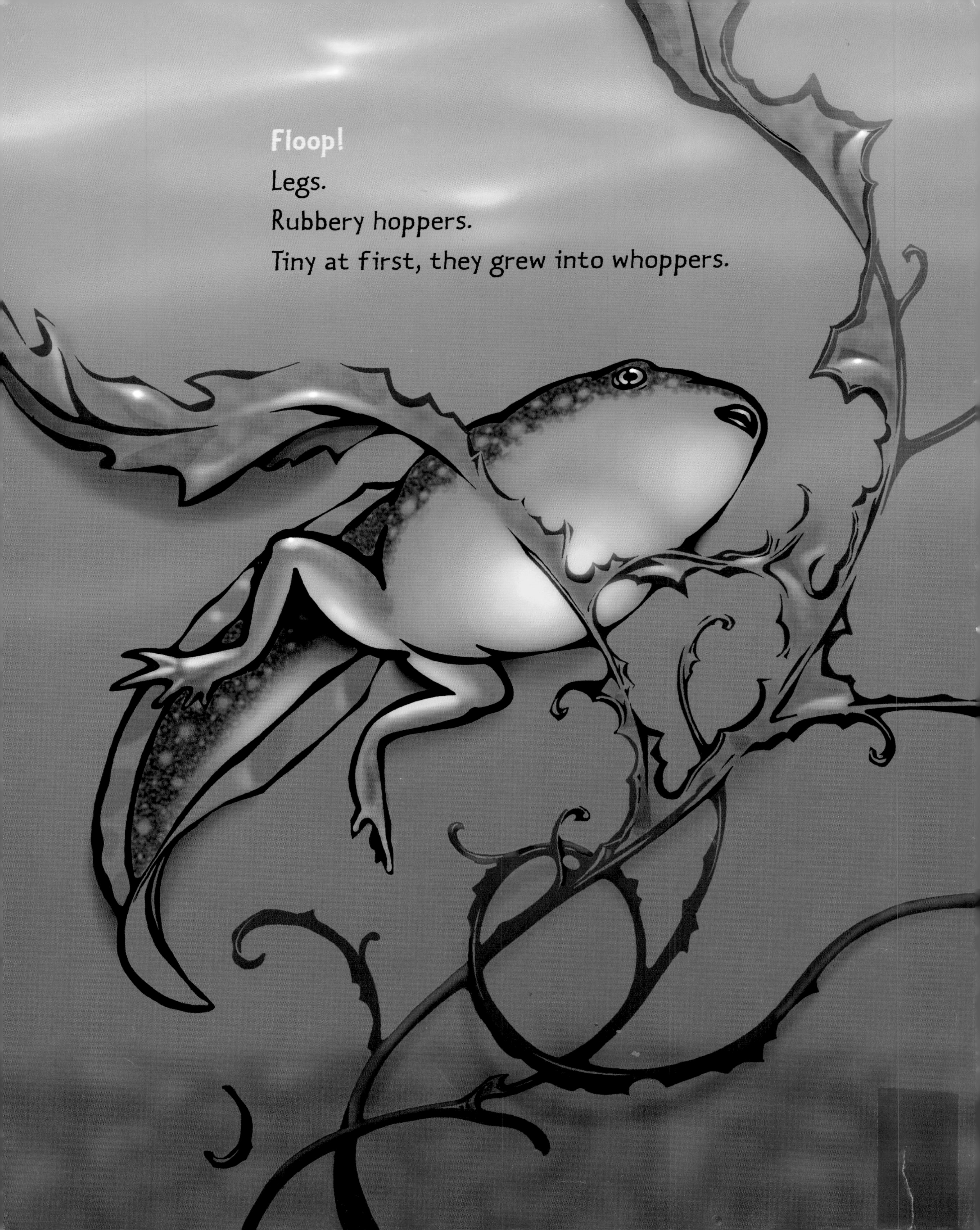

Floop!

Legs.

Rubbery hoppers.

Tiny at first, they grew into whoppers.

Fleep!

Arms.

Supple and bendable.

Not very strong, but still, dependable.

Patience and time. That's all it took.

Suddenly Rex had a whole new look.

Rex didn't hide in the goop anymore.
Out came his inner tyrannosaur!

Inflating his throat and lifting his head,
Rex gave a roar—

Ribbet! he said.

Lumbering duckbills were taken aback
to see an amphibian on the attack.

Alamosauruses craned their necks
to get a good look at Tadpole Rex.

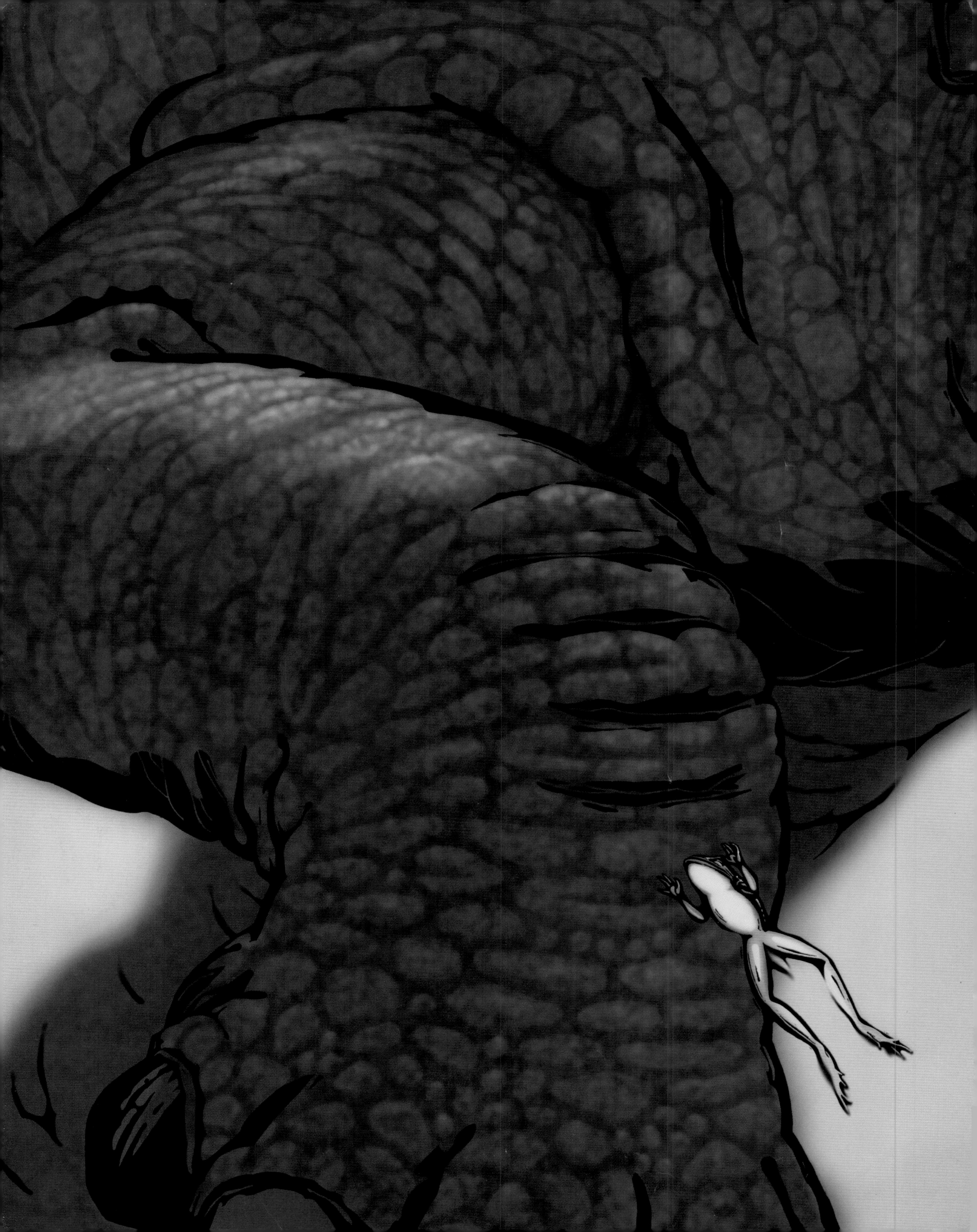

Bouncing about with the boldest of hops,
Rex nearly tripped a triceratops.

Stomp! went the dinosaur.
Squish! went the goop.
Ribbet! went Rex.
Bloop.
Bloop.
Bloop.

Rex hunkered down with a gulp and a grin,
his inner tyrannosaur corked within.

Two blinking eyes. That's all he let show,
watching the dinosaurs come and go.

Gone are the dinosaurs. Gone are the stompers,
the rippers, the roarers, the bone-crunching chompers.
Gone are the dinosaurs, swept away. . . .

But hoppers and croakers are here to stay.

Tree frogs and bullfrogs and little spring peepers,
sure-footed climbers and long-distance leapers.
Frogs of all fashions continue to huddle
around any suitable freshwater puddle.

And somewhere inside,
deep in their core,
they *all* have an inner
tyrannosaur.

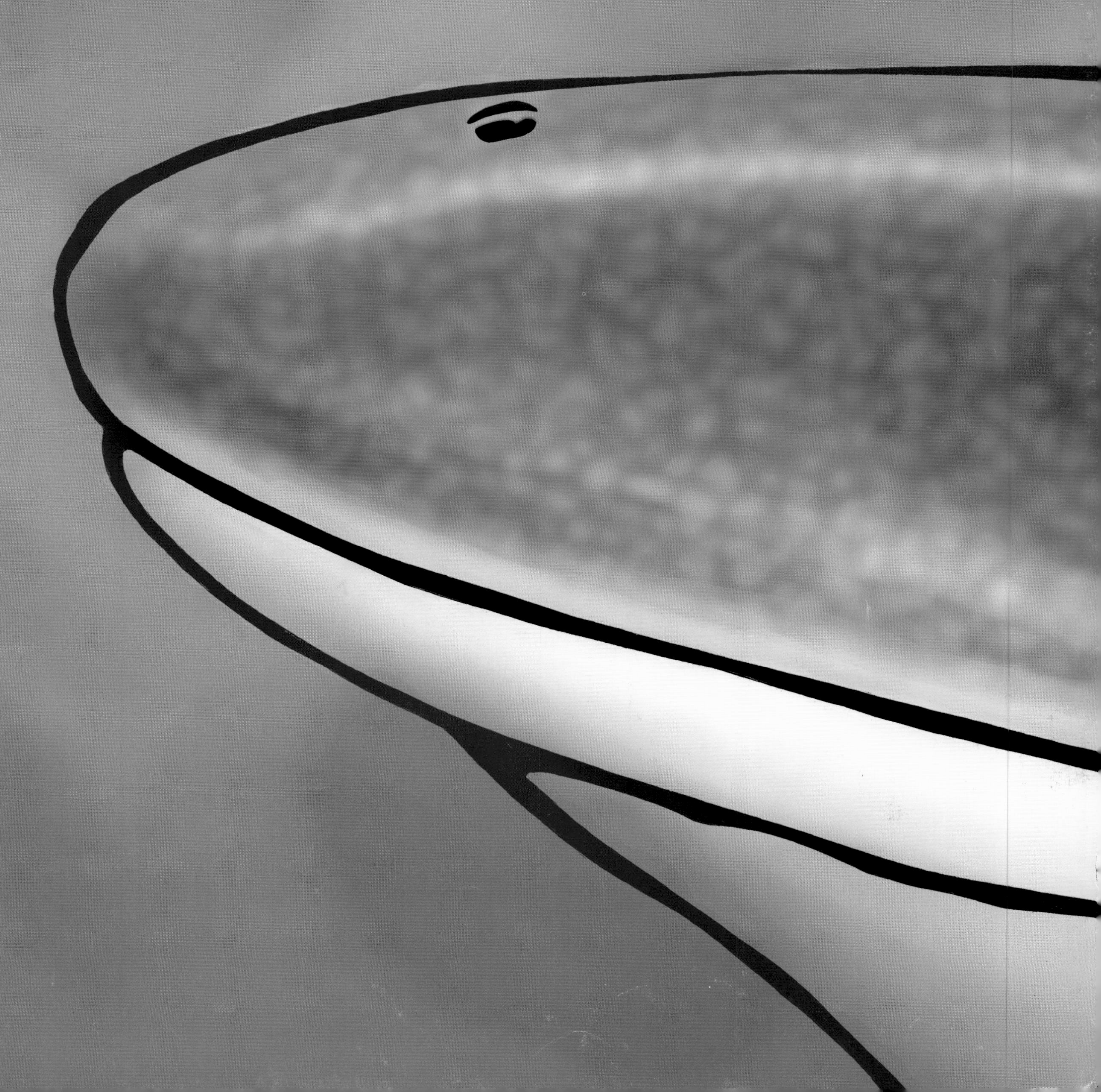

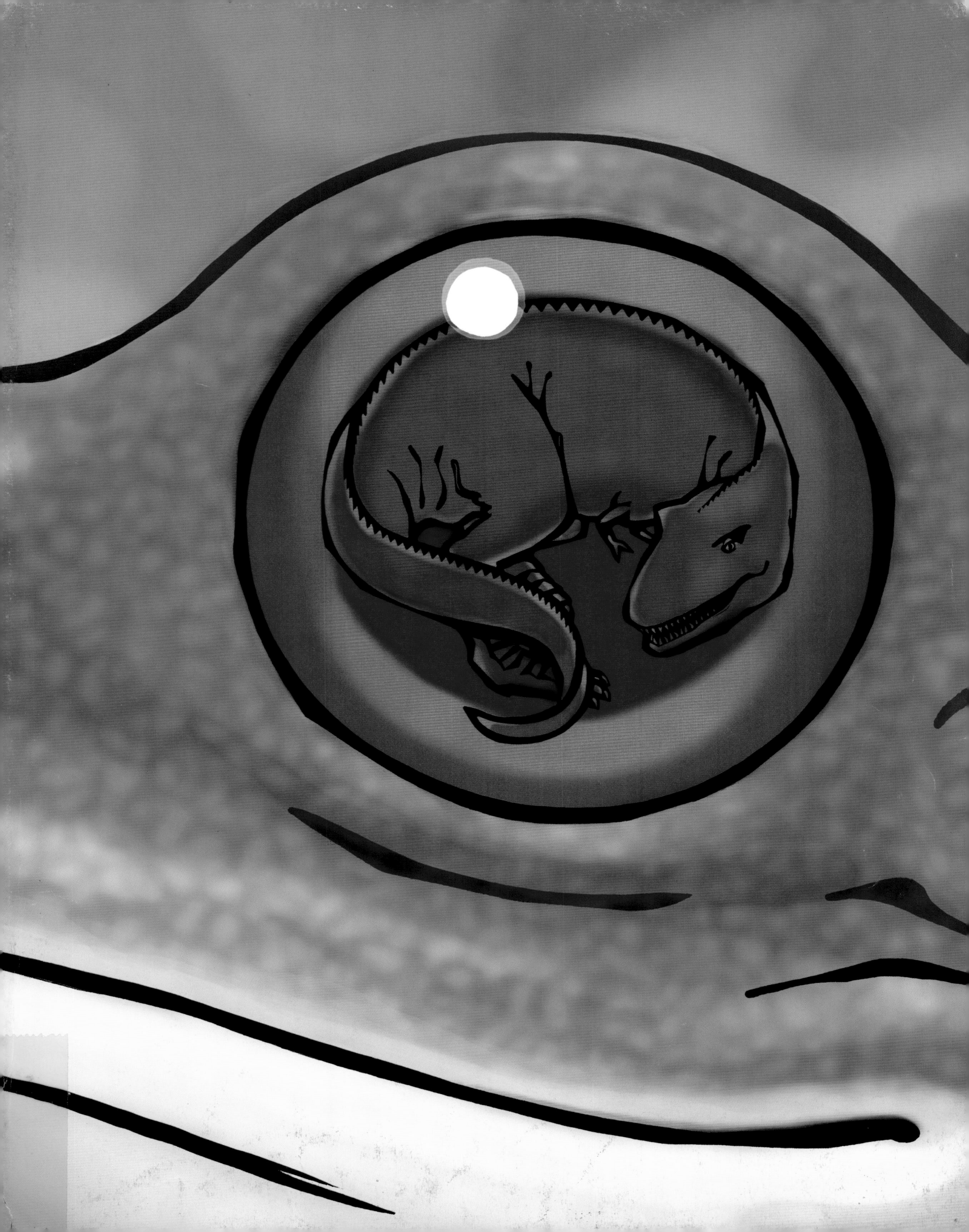

Does a tadpole really have an inner tyrannosaur? Yes . . . in a way. When a tadpole becomes a frog, it does more than grow limbs and lose its tail. Unseen changes take place inside as well. Gills are replaced by lungs so the frog can live on land. At the same time, its digestive system transforms. The plant-eating tadpole becomes a meat-eating frog. When Rex emerges from his puddle in this story, he is hungry for live prey—just like a tyrannosaur.

Frogs really did live alongside tyrannosaurs and triceratops. In fact, frogs existed 100 million years *before* these particular dinosaurs evolved. Fossils show that some prehistoric frogs had short legs, while others had long. Some had wide heads, others narrow. And many, like Rex, had well-developed teeth. Frogs came in all shapes and sizes, just as they do today.

After 200 million years on Earth, frogs now find their world changing rapidly. New challenges—pollution, habitat loss, climate change—are taking a severe toll. As scientists search for solutions to these problems, we can hope that hoppers and croakers will be around to enrich ecosystems for many more millions of years.

Many thanks to Linnea

www.HarcourtBooks.com

Library of Congress Cataloging-in-Publication Data
Cyrus, Kurt.
Tadpole Rex/Kurt Cyrus.
p. cm.
Summary: A tiny primordial tadpole grows into a frog, feeling just as strong and powerful as the huge tyrannosaurus rex that stomps through the mud.
[1. Tadpoles—Fiction. 2. Frogs—Fiction. 3. Dinosaurs—Fiction. 4. Growth—Fiction. 5. Stories in rhyme.]
I. Title.
PZ8.3.C997Tad 2008
[E]—dc22 2006033825
ISBN 978-0-15-205990-3

First edition
A C E G H F D B

Manufactured in China

The illustrations in this book were done in scratchboard and then colored digitally.
The display type was set in House of Terror.
The text type was set in Kosmik Plain One.
Color separations by Bright Arts Ltd., Hong Kong
Manufactured by South China Printing Company, Ltd., China
Production supervision by Christine Witnik
Designed by Linda Lockowitz